Today's date:

Scripture:

Reflections:

Prayers:

Today's date:

Scripture:

Reflections:

Prayers:

Today's date:

Scripture:

Reflections:

Prayers:

Today's date:

Scripture:

Reflections:

Prayers:

Today's date:

Scripture:

Reflections:

Prayers:

Today's date:

Scripture:

Reflections:

Prayers:

Today's date:

Scripture:

Reflections:

Prayers:

Today's date:

Scripture:

Reflections:

Prayers:

Today's date:

Scripture:

Reflections:

Prayers:

Today's date:

Scripture:

Reflections:

Prayers:

Today's date:

Scripture:

Reflections:

Prayers:

Today's date:

Scripture:

Reflections:

Prayers:

Today's date:

Scripture:

Reflections:

Prayers:

Today's date:

Scripture:

Reflections:

Prayers:

Today's date:

Scripture:

Reflections:

Prayers:

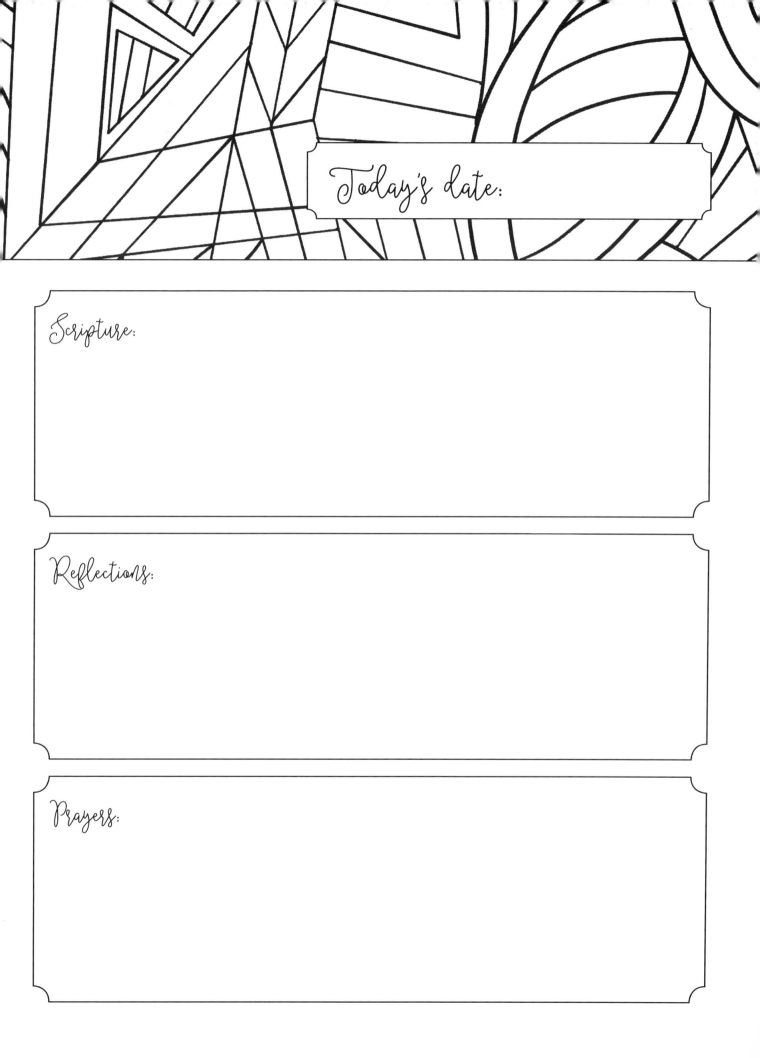

Today's date:

Scripture:

Reflections:

Prayers:

Today's date:

Scripture:

Reflections:

Prayers:

Today's date:

Scripture:

Reflections:

Prayers:

Today's date:

Scripture:

Reflections:

Prayers:

Today's date:

Scripture:

Reflections:

Prayers:

Today's date:

Scripture:

Reflections:

Prayers:

Today's date:

Scripture:

Reflections:

Prayers:

Today's date:

Scripture:

Reflections:

Prayers:

Today's date:

Scripture:

Reflections:

Prayers:

Today's date:

Scripture:

Reflections:

Prayers:

Today's date:

Scripture:

Reflections:

Prayers:

Today's date:

Scripture:

Reflections:

Prayers:

Today's date:

Scripture:

Reflections:

Prayers:

Today's date:

Scripture:

Reflections:

Prayers:

Today's date:

Scripture:

Reflections:

Prayers:

Today's date:

Scripture:

Reflections:

Prayers:

Today's date:

Scripture:

Reflections:

Prayers:

Today's date:

Scripture:

Reflections:

Prayers:

Today's date:

Scripture:

Reflections:

Prayers:

Today's date:

Scripture:

Reflections:

Prayers:

Today's date:

Scripture:

Reflections:

Prayers:

Today's date:

Scripture:

Reflections:

Prayers:

Today's date:

Scripture:

Reflections:

Prayers:

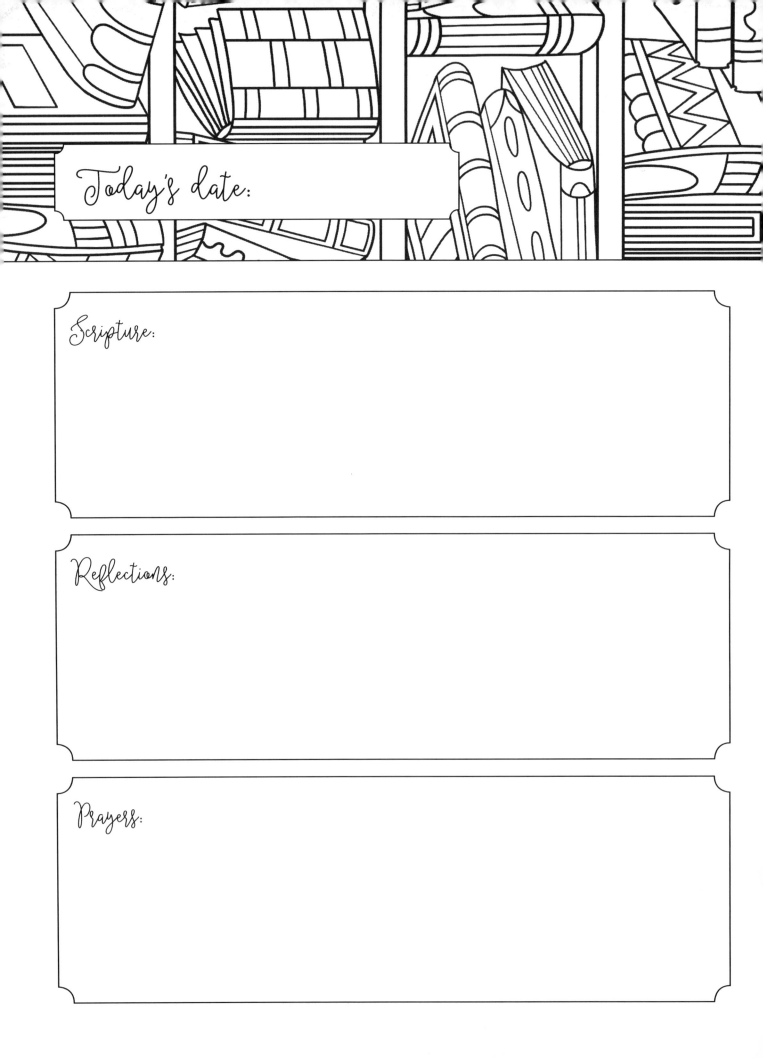

Today's date:

Scripture:

Reflections:

Prayers:

Today's date:

Scripture:

Reflections:

Prayers:

Today's date:

Scripture:

Reflections:

Prayers:

Today's date:

Scripture:

Reflections:

Prayers:

Today's date:

Scripture:

Reflections:

Prayers:

Today's date:

Scripture:

Reflections:

Prayers:

Today's date:

Scripture:

Reflections:

Prayers:

Today's date:

Scripture:

Reflections:

Prayers:

Today's date:

Scripture:

Reflections:

Prayers:

Today's date:

Scripture:

Reflections:

Prayers:

Today's date:

Scripture:

Reflections:

Prayers:

Today's date:

Scripture:

Reflections:

Prayers:

Today's date:

Scripture:

Reflections:

Prayers:

Today's date:

Scripture:

Reflections:

Prayers:

Today's date:

Scripture:

Reflections:

Prayers:

Today's date:

Scripture:

Reflections:

Prayers:

Today's date:

Scripture:

Reflections:

Prayers:

Today's date:

Scripture:

Reflections:

Prayers:

Today's date:

Scripture:

Reflections:

Prayers:

Today's date:

Scripture:

Reflections:

Prayers:

Today's date:

Scripture:

Reflections:

Prayers:

Today's date:

Scripture:

Reflections:

Prayers:

Today's date:

Scripture:

Reflections:

Prayers:

Today's date:

Scripture:

Reflections:

Prayers:

Today's date:

Scripture:

Reflections:

Prayers:

Today's date:

Scripture:

Reflections:

Prayers:

Today's date:

Scripture:

Reflections:

Prayers:

Today's date:

Scripture:

Reflections:

Prayers:

Today's date:

Scripture:

Reflections:

Prayers:

Today's date:

Scripture:

Reflections:

Prayers:

Today's date:

Scripture:

Reflections:

Prayers:

Today's date:

Scripture:

Reflections:

Prayers:

Today's date:

Scripture:

Reflections:

Prayers:

Today's date:

Scripture:

Reflections:

Prayers:

Today's date:

Scripture:

Reflections:

Prayers:

Today's date:

Scripture:

Reflections:

Prayers:

Today's date:

Scripture:

Reflections:

Prayers:

Today's date:

Scripture:

Reflections:

Prayers:

Today's date:

Scripture:

Reflections:

Prayers:

Today's date:

Scripture:

Reflections:

Prayers:

Made in the USA
Lexington, KY
13 November 2018